The truth is that we must number Venice
among the 'cities of the soul'…
she has the fatal gift to touch the imagination,
to awaken a permanent desire.

Horatio F. Brown

Venice
A day in Carnival

This book is dedicated to
Fiona, Tristan & Danièle

Photographs by

MICHAEL LUCAS

Venice
A day in Carnival

ARCPERIPLUS

© Arcperiplus Publishing Ltd, 2004

© Photographs by Michael Lucas 2004

© Essay by Raphäele Vidaling 2004

First published in October 2004 by

Arcperiplus Publishing Ltd

The Sorting Office

21 Station Road

London SW13 0LF

PUBLISHER: Danièle Juncqua Naveau

DESIGN: Linda Wade

MANAGING EDITOR: Nick Easterbrook

PRODUCTION MANAGER: Sophie Chéry

PRODUCTION ASSISTANT: Arvind Shah

ISBN 1-902699-61-0

Scanning and reprographics, Periplus Publishing London Ltd

Film Processing: Fleshtone Color Lab

Printed and bound in Italy by Graphicom

Contents

Venice
Introduction

Introduction
Michael Lucas

I arrived in Venice by air with friends who had visited
Venice before. We would see no cars, or any other non-
aquatic forms of transportation, for the duration of our
visit. We left the modern airport, and prepared to step
into the past. At my friends' suggestion we took a water
taxi from the airport. I highly recommend this for the
first time visitor, and it should not be confused with the
conventional taxi experience. It is disconcerting to wheel
one's luggage-laden cart out of the airport terminal to
the water's edge and the bobbing transportation waiting
there. The boat was sleek and classical, and owing to
three million coats of varnish, gave the appearance of
being made entirely of glass. Safely on board, you could
not be further from a four-wheeled cab; you wonder:
will we dine at the captain's table tonight? Given the

second mortgage you need to pay the fare, it doesn't seem an unreasonable request. Still, now is not the time to think of such things. The captain engages the monster engines and we move slowly into the estuary. We make for the marked channel, and as soon as we enter it the captain opens up the engines to Mach speed. We are exhilarated, and no one speaks. At this speed it's actually not possible to speak, at least no one would hear you. We pass the island cemetery of San Michele – the dead centre of town.

It was February. The water-laden air, heavy and cold, diffused and saturated the colours. The light really was different. Everyone talked about 'the light', I wasn't sure if this was it, though. As we left the estuary, the captain slowed our craft to enter the small canals of Venice. My first impression of Venetian housing was that it could be charitably described as, well, rustic. Many houses were replete with wild collections of drying washing, hung from every conceivable vertical surface. We now motored slowly past the ancient arsenal, and towards the last bridge and the end of the canal. I had the distinct feeling that my friends were

stealing looks in my direction, as if anticipating the result of some prank. We cleared the last bridge and entered the lagoon.

The shock forced me to sit down heavily in the boat. Venice is beautiful! I sat awe-struck, absorbing Venice through every pore of my body. What I did not do though, was record this experience on film. I couldn't bring myself to place any object between my eyes and this wonderful vision. Such was my introduction to Venice, and the start of a life-long love affair.

The images in this book were taken over a decade ago, but like Venice, they seem timeless. The city does not need novelties, but we had arrived during Carnival, and the city was made more enticing and friendly because of it. Carnival is the world's most extravagant fancy-dress party. Some of the wild and surreal costumes are in stark contrast with the city's culture and history. But as unlikely as it seems, it works. In fact, it adds yet another photographic dimension to the world's most photogenic city.

So on my first day, I set forth with my camera, rather like a child who has been accidentally locked inside a large and lavish toy store. The night before I could not sleep, and rose early, much too early. Possibly a combination of childish anticipation and adult jet lag. I found myself standing in St Mark's Square, cold and in the dark. I stood for two hours before there was enough light to take even the longest of long exposures. As I waited, a romantic notion occurred to me. In this place, and at this time, I was sharing the anticipation of the day's first light, the same anticipation felt perhaps by Turner and Canaletto. The light comes gradually, blue at first, then with a little more colour; images diffused in the mist. The light strengthened, and hit the water, creating diamonds that began to dance, and then, so did I.

Michael Lucas
2004

Venice
La Serenissima

La Serenissima
Raphäele Vidaling

In three days, it will be summer. It's not so hot here in Krakow, and yet Henri is sweating in his bed. He hears a creaking in the room; he jumps. Are they here already? He again glances through the letter that his mother, Marie de' Medici, has sent him: King Charles IX is dead, he needs to get himself back to Paris as fast as possible. For he, now, is King of France…

It is 18 June 1574, and Henri III has gone to bed still fully clothed. He has reigned over Poland for 120 days and fears he may be stuck here for a long time to come. Hence this decision to leave like a thief in the night. More noise; whispers… Ah yes, it's Villequier and du Gast, his companions, who've slipped in. "The horses are ready in the courtyard. We need to get a move on." They immediately make their getaway, without luggage and without noise. Without luggage? No: with a thief's bulging doublet containing the diamonds of the Polish crown, which they have just purloined.

Henri III is 23 years old. For a whole month he will gallop towards Paris, via Austria – towards his royal future. What could be more urgent? And yet, on 17 July, he cannot resist an invitation from the Doge of Venice, like Ulysses, in a hurry to get back to Ithaca and yet lingering in the arms of Circe and Calypso.

Venice? The King has heard of it, of course. Who hasn't heard of Venice? It's the city of freedom and festivities, the most luxurious shop window for art in the western world, the most powerful bank, the biggest commercial entrepot in Europe, the first modern police state, able to keep Islam at bay and negotiate on equal terms with the kingdom of France and the Holy Roman Empire. They say that the 16,000 workers in the arsenal are capable of constructing and arming a galley in little more than a day! Three years earlier, the Christian fleet, half of it Venetian, was able to send to the bottom 100 Turkish galleys, their hulls smashed and their oars broken. How could Henri III ever forget the famous

Battle of Lepanto? Nobody at this time speaks of the anachronistic charm of a moribund city: Venice is at the apogee of its glory, coveted a thousand times and never vanquished.

The young King is expected at Marghera, on *terra firma*, by 60 senators. From among a whole fleet of gondolas, three are offered him to choose between, just as in fairy stories: the first one is draped in black velvet, another in purple velvet and the third in gold cloth. As in the fairy tales, he chooses the gondola in gold, which eight rowers in satin skirts will soon take out to the island of Murano. But the most magical sight is yet to come: the discovery of Venice itself, its banquets and its spectacles, its official ceremonies and its nocturnal escapades. Succumbing entirely to its charm, he will remain in the 'red city' until the beginning of September, and when he leaves, his arms will be full of presents and purchases – including over 1,000 écus' worth of musk.

And then, there's something else in his luggage. Not stolen jewels, this time, nor even a carnival mask. An unexpected souvenir of Venice, that the tourist

boutiques wouldn't dream of trying to sell these days. Something so common that nobody is aware of its Venetian origin. Something that everyone has in their kitchen… A fork!

That little pronged instrument may date back originally to Egyptian times, but Venetians credit its invention to the wife of Doge Domenico Selvo in 1070. The whim of an elegant woman, and one which found few imitators during the Middle Ages, or even later: however noble a person may have been, they ate with their fingers. Catherine de' Medici, known for her greed, never abandoned the practice. And yet Henri III was about to sow the seeds of a small revolution in the history of eating when he brought back his Venetian fork. Soon, the fashion for wearing enormous ruffs was to justify this import: there was no gainsaying the practicality of this new accessory.

Why begin this trip to Venice with the story of Henri III? It's a matter of chance, or almost. We could have taken almost any great man from almost any era: not one would have escaped the allure of Venice, any more than the sailors in the *Odyssey* could escape the sirens' song, or the power of the witch Circe. Equally bewitching, Venice is a magical place to stop off. Few people actually live there (hence the drama of the modern city, which so many are leaving: "there are fewer of us than there are pigeons," the natives lament), but everyone passes through it.

Venice was the scene for the love affair between George Sand and Alfred de Musset. It was here that Lord Byron wrote his *Don Juan*, Wagner his *Parsifal* and Hemingway his semi-autobiography, and here that Aragon tried to commit suicide. This was the site of the key scene of Proust's 'uneven paving stones', in *Time Regained*, a title which suits the city so well. It was the backdrop chosen by Thomas Mann for the death of his old poet, obsessed by the young Tadzio, in a story that would fascinate Visconti. Here too are buried Ezra Pound, Stravinsky and Diaghilev...

Everyone goes to Venice at least once in their lives. They never come back disappointed, so long as they take the trouble to venture off the crowded tourist tracks just a little. Even the sceptical, the world-weary, the fastidious, the not-in-the-least-in-love, the bored-with-travelling, the people allergic to clichés, and the ones left cold by picture postcard views and the promises of travel brochures, are not indifferent to the charms of Venice, and cannot return disappointed from a trip there. That's how it is. Napoleon Bonaparte threatened the rebellious city that he would be 'the Attila of Venice'. He went on to steal the famous horses of St Mark's to adorn the triumphal arch of the Carrousel in Paris (they were returned in 1815). He availed himself of a few other souvenirs, but didn't strip the city of its thousand and one attractions.

So, why mention the story of the fork? It's merely one little-known detail: there is no fork museum in Venice and the city possesses many other more eloquent symbols, including the lion, the cat and the gondola. The princess's little fork is just one of numerous legends, more or less authentic, that have flourished in the mud of this magical city. One further proof, in short, that Venice is more than the sum of its clichés – the city is a veritable reservoir of surprises.

Locals claim there isn't a map of the city that is complete: test them yourself – on each one there'll be an alley missing, or a bridge, or a path will lead to a dead-end abruptly closed off by a gate that isn't mentioned anywhere. Its legendary dimension is more or less similar to that twisting and turning topography, which no cartographer's rigour can capture. No one has ever surveyed all the legends about Venice that are in circulation – legends about certain of its palaces, certain of its districts, certain of the (masked) characters who have wandered through its maze of canals and *calli* (alleys).

What, for instance, happened to the clockmakers who devised the mechanism for the great clock and the automata on the Torre dell'Orologio (Clock Tower), to the north of St Mark's Square? They had their eyes put out, to guarantee that Venice alone would have the benefit of their work.

Did Marco Polo really go to China? All that we know of this great Venetian traveller is what he recounts of China in his *Book of Marvels*, dictated in prison to the writer known as Rusticiano of Pisa. He doesn't mention foot-binding, the tea ceremony, pictograms, paper, porcelain or even the Great Wall. Did he make it all up?

Why are the houses of Burano so brightly coloured? According to legend, the fishermen's wives would wait for their menfolk in front of their houses, and wave to their returning boats. But through the *caligo*, the fog which habitually envelops the lagoon at nightfall, nothing looked more like your wife's hand than your neighbour's wife's hand. So the distinctive colour of each façade was meant to distinguish between the houses, as well as to brighten up a watery landscape melting into melancholy fog.

Finally, did you know that the word and concept of 'ghetto' were invented in Venice? In Italian, *geto* means foundry. And it was to the site of a previous cannon foundry, today the Cannaregio district, that the Jews were suddenly restricted by a decree of 29 March 1516. Jewish merchants had arrived in the region at the start of the 14th century, and at first had been refused the right of settling in the city. While they could trade in the port, they nonetheless had to live on *terra firma*. When the troops of the League of Cambrai disembarked in 1508 (this was an alliance formed between Pope Julius II, Emperor Maximilian, the King of France Louis XII, and Ferdinand of Aragon, against the Republic of Venice), the Jewish merchants took refuge in the city, which finally tolerated their presence – especially that of their money, which helped to finance the war. But eight years later, they decided that enough was enough: the Republic decreed that the Jews would henceforth be obliged "to go straightaway and inhabit all together in the block of houses situated in the Geto Nuevo […] To prevent them circulating at night, two gates will be set up, opened at dawn and closed at midnight." However, despite this discrimination, a once unhealthy district saw the birth of a sort of republic within the Republic, with a European-wide reputation for its doctors, its clothing workshops and its Talmudic schools. The real problem was still the confined space to which the community was restricted: from 700 inhabitants in 1516, it leapt to 50,000 by the end of the 17th century! Hence the unusual height of the buildings in the district, that frequently reach six, seven, eight or even nine storeys. Only with the arrival of Bonaparte, in 1797, were the gates of the ghetto destroyed. But the word remained.

Long is the list of stories both great and small that have marked the 'unnatural city', as Chateaubriand called it. Its origins, to begin with. The legend speaks of a city built on the water to flee 'the divine scourge'. As if, once you were off dry land, you could escape from God's gaze and punishment. For there is something of the Tower of Babel in the genesis of Venice: the same sin of pride on the part of a handful of mortals who wanted to defy simultaneously the laws of physics and architecture (by building on the water) and the laws of time (for a lagoon is by definition temporary: either it ends up being filled in, or the sea beaks through the coastal barrier and swallows it up). Venice is thus a sort of gigantic wager against time: the proof that something ephemeral can last for at least 15 centuries! And yet, the 'divine scourges' have not spared it – from the high tides regularly capable of covering St Mark's (the *acqua alta* of 1966 filled the entire world with alarm) to clouds of insects, not forgetting the Black Death…

So, if the legend speaks of the inhabitants fleeing the divine scourge, history for its part tells rather of them fleeing before the arrival of the barbarian hordes from the north: the Lombard invasions. Already rebellious, Venice was built not so much on water as on a single word that was to serve as its slogan: 'No!' The first Venetes, and the Venetians subsequently, would over the centuries share this obstinate will to defend their independence. Remember, after all, the name of the bridge that leads to the island nowadays: the Bridge of Liberty… A small group of fishermen and salt merchants were probably already occupying the site, but the new arrivals, at the time of the invasions, were intent on building a city. So their resistance also had implications for their way of life. The barbarians were nomads; they claimed, in response, to be sedentary. They thus created a real city, built to last, even if it was built on water! To celebrate this birth, they set aside the date of 25 March – St Mark's day.

'Built on water' is in any case a manner of speaking, since the city rests on the *terra firma* of hundreds of islands and islets (118, to be precise), upon which constructions were simply 'propped up' by millions of wooden stakes. For this purpose, whole forests of oak and larch were imported from the Alps. According to archaeological studies, certain stakes are over a thousand years old. As for the number of them, it makes you giddy: 10,000 were necessary to support the Rialto Bridge alone, 100,000 were used for St Mark's campanile, and over a million to build the Salute!

And lo and behold, this little town that sprang out of nowhere, and that should have sunk without trace long ago, became, in the 13th century, with its 100,000 inhabitants, the third city in Europe, after Paris and Naples. It was the third from a demographic point of view, but in the economic arena it surpassed itself, becoming the marketplace of the world. The West provided it with wood, metal, wool, hemp and linen cloth, honey, fur and finished luxury articles (mirrors, candelabra, paper). Venice traded in return sugar, spices, perfumes, slaves, silks, cottons, alum and dyes imported from the East.

So how can we explain the miracle of this perpetual reprieve? It's quite simple, Venetians will tell you: it's all thanks to St Mark. The story goes that one day the evangelist was shipwrecked in the lagoon, where he founded the church of Aquileia, which gave birth to the patriarchate of Venice. Having taken refuge on the site of the present basilica, he heard an angel speak these words, which can still be read on the escutcheons of the Venetian Republic: "Peace be with you, Mark my evangelist; it is here that your bones will rest." There's no point in arguing with an angel. And yet there was one thing that for a long time needled the Venetians, to whom this honour had been promised – the fact that Mark had later become the first bishop of Alexandria, and had died there. Even worse, the city of Alexandria, in the 7th century, fell under Muslim authority, which was not much inclined to listen to angels. Whatever was to become of the saint's relics?

The story is well worth the telling. In the 9th century, Venice and Alexandria were among the great crossroads of Mediterranean trade; they kept up good commercial relations. Two merchants of Venice, Buono de Malmocco and Rustico de Torcello, happened to be in Alexandria when they learned that the caliph there was in the process of stripping all the churches in the city of their treasures. The two merchants were immediately filled with anxiety about the relics of St Mark, which

risked profanation, or being lost forever. They suggested that the priests put the body on board their boat for safekeeping; our merchants in fact had the intention of weighing anchor and 'forgetting' to return the goods on board. The priests demurred. Why sell a hen that lays golden eggs?

After all, relics, at this time, constituted a profitable market. The numerous pilgrims gave offerings to have access to them and the Church – strangely enough – was far from averse to them. Profits of this kind imply trafficking: the commerce of relics, in the Middle Ages, was as active as it was forbidden. Anyone practising it was accused of simony (the sale of spiritual goods), but the gains were well worth the risk. The populace was demanding, and ready to pay itinerant demonstrators to see and touch the toes of St Catherine (preserved, in Venice, at San Giovanni e Paolo), the teeth of St Stephen, three threads of Christ's swaddling clothes, the milk of the Blessed Virgin, a plank from Noah's Ark, twigs from the Burning Bush, or even a fragment of the rod of Moses – so they said! Charlemagne himself always wore round his neck a fragment of the One True

Cross... and the only true thing about this was probably its name, since 1150 fragments could be counted throughout the world – enough, if you assembled all the fragments, to constitute, according to Calvin, "the cargo of a huge boat."

After long confabulations, our two zealous merchants managed to recover the coveted body. Two challenges remained: they needed to get past the Muslim guards and the customs. To dupe the former, they buried the body at the bottom of a chest and covered it with layers of pork, a meat considered taboo by the Muslims. Protected by ham, the holy relics thus slipped through the net. To escape the customs, they resorted to another stratagem: the body, enveloped in its shroud, was wrapped in the sails, after which it was plain sailing.

Once they arrived in Venice, our heroes still had a few anxieties. What if here too they were to be accused of simony? After all, even though they had been working for the good of the whole city, they had employed some fairly unorthodox means. Would they be acclaimed by the crowd or thrown into prison, shut away for instance in the cells high up on the campanile,

now replaced by the stairs that are climbed by floods of tourists? An envoy is sent to test the waters. Doge Partecipazio welcomes them with open arms, together with Bishop Orso. A glorious day for the city: Venice has got its patron saint back.

The story doesn't quite end there. The relics were first placed in a corner of the Doge's Palace for safekeeping while a church was erected in their honour. The new basilica was built between 1063 and 1094. But when the time came to transfer the relics they were not to be found! The mosaics, admired every day by thousands of visitors and responsible for the nickname of 'the golden church', relate in images the rest of the adventure: St Mark himself raised his arm from a pillar to reveal his hiding place. On 8 October 1094, the transfer of the relics finally took place, in great pomp and circumstance. Nothing serious could now befall Venice, since the saint had been returned to his proper place…

Of St Mark there remains the basilica dedicated to him, now the cathedral of Venice, and the square of the same name, one of the most famous in the world, the only one in the city to be called a *piazza*, whereas the others have to content themselves with being a *campo* or a *campiello*. And then there is also the lion, the evangelist's emblem in the same way as the eagle is the emblem of St John, the angel of St Matthew or the bull of St Luke. His gilded statue, dating from 1170, perched atop his column, is apparently a chimera of Chinese or Persian origin, to which artisans of the Middle Ages added wings. On the façade of the Doge's Palace, among other places, the lion is represented with one paw resting on an open Bible bearing the inscription: "Pax tibi Marce Evangelista meus," emphasising the peace that Venice could assure its territories. In times of war, conversely, the lion was depicted holding a sword over a closed book, alluding to the determination of the city and its military might.

Finally, as is less well known, the lion in Venice also gives its name to the *Bocca del Leone*, 'the lion's maw', a letterbox placed in every district in the city (there is still one in the court of the Doge's Palace), into which citizens were invited to post letters denouncing the enemies of the Republic. These denunciations, as often as not anonymous, were examined by the Council of

Ten, which would take the necessary measures: they would summon suspects to the attics of the Doge's Palace, where the Murder Bureau was responsible for dealing with rebels. Few governments have taken as far as Venice the surveillance not only of its subjects, but of its own members. The best example is doubtless the execution of Doge Marin Falier on 17 April 1355. Despite the fact that he was a doge, he was decapitated for having hatched a plot against the government. You can still visit not only the New Prisons, linked to the Doge's Palace by the famous Bridge of (Last) Sighs, but also the torture chambers and the *pozzi*, damp wells into which prisoners were thrown.

Today, while there are still numerous sculpted stone lions (14 in St Mark's Square alone), the felines that you encounter at every street corner are cats! It is impossible to imagine the city without the presence of these animals, silent, elegant and elusive, just as the city herself is. You see them in some dead-end alley, a dozen or so of them, hunkered round a plate of spaghetti that some kindly soul has set on the ground for them. These kindly souls are most frequently women, called by the locals *mamme dei gatti*, the 'cats' mothers'. Stray cats also have an ultra-modern reception centre at their disposal, on the sea-front of the Lido, while a specialist bookshop is dedicated to the beloved feline. In Venice, indeed, the cat is practically venerated as a god. To kill one, says the tradition, is to condemn yourself to die within the year.

Why are they treated with such esteem? The reason is that, among the scourges that have assailed the city, the gravest, which decimated tens of thousands of people, was the plague. In 1348, it killed over a third of the population of Venice. In 1576, it was still ravaging the city, carrying off among others the famous painter known as Titian, real name Tiziano Vecellio, the portraitist of the greatest men and women of Europe, who dominated Venetian painting throughout the 16th century. In 1630, there was a new deadly epidemic. The doctors didn't know which way to turn – their heads covered by those characteristic great masks shaped like birds' beaks, which they thought protected them from the deadly miasma. They were quite useless, of course. The only way to prevent the spread of the disease was to

eradicate the rats, the main carriers. But there were huge numbers of these rats in this crossroads of Mediterranean commerce, with its granaries filled with edible merchandise. For this purpose, nothing was more effective than the cat. Brought from the East, where it was already venerated as a 'purifying' hunter, especially in Egypt, where it was domesticated for the first time, it ensured that Venice was protected from rodents. Today you can find every breed of cat, but the most emblematic is the surián, that beige or tawny cat with its striped coat. As for angoras, the legend says that they were imported for the first time into Europe by Armenians from the island of San Lazzaro.

Of all domestic animals, cats are probably the most independent, the ones most enamoured of liberty… just like the Venetians. And this is so even though their liberty is bounded by the sea all around. As they are imprisoned by the water, the cats thus reproduce *intra muros*, in what was for a long time an island: the railway bridge leading to Venice was only built in 1846, and the road bridge in 1933. And when you see how narrow some of the alleys are – so narrow you can't even open an umbrella – you reflect that the labyrinth was built to the scale of these furry little predators...

To the maze of the streets and alleys corresponds the maze of the canals, straddled by the 400 or so bridges in the city. All originally in wood, including the Rialto, they were often private property. So you had to pay a toll to use them – a toll which didn't include all-risk insurance. And yet people frequently fell into the water, since the bridges had no hand rails (the local newspaper the *Gazzettino* enjoys publishing a daily list of people who fall in). Hence the famous combats that took place on the arches of the bridges, between rival families. Some of the bridges retain a memory of this in their names, like the Ponte dei Pugni (Bridge of Fists) and the Ponte della Guerra (Bridge of War), where two clans that had always been rivals, the Nicolotti and the Castellani, would confront each other. For the crowd this may have been an enjoyable spectacle, but for the belligerents it was a veritable battle, in which many of them met their deaths. The government, faithful to the idea of 'dividing and conquering', encouraged these habits, and even organised them as a form of

entertainment when foreign dignitaries came to visit. A similar show was put on for Henri III: scandalised by such violence, he demanded that these practices be abolished. This didn't happen until 1705.

Venice is a city of spectacle, a city which shows itself off, a city for curious spectators from the entire world. The palaces possess ostentatious facades only on the 'public' side, the one that overlooks the canal, while the rear facades, overlooking the courtyard or the street, are unadorned. These rich palaces, in spite of the diversity of their ornamentation, are almost all built on a plan that survives every change in fashion: that of the house/entrepot, or *casa fondego* – an inevitable result of maritime commerce. The ground floor, on the water level, is made up of a landing pontoon, warehouses and offices. The first storey is called the *piano nobile*: these are the luxurious rooms, the 'noble' rooms, where great festivities are held. The family's living spaces properly speaking are on the third storey, while the servants and the kitchen are relegated to the attic. Trading, feasting and family life: the three great storeys of a house and the three great axes of the Venetian life-style.

While bridge fights and other games (human pyramids, regattas, etc.) are inherent to Venice, the greatest spectacle is obviously the Carnival, a participatory event of a kind modernity itself could never have invented, "a festival that the people gives to itself, and not one that is given to the people," as Goethe wrote – and this was at least originally true. It is likely that the carnival tradition dates back to the 11th century, though the first written reference we have to it is from 1268. This mention is a decree forbidding young patricians from throwing eggs at women. We know that these eggs were sometimes filled with rose water… and sometimes with less pleasant fluids. What are we to imagine lay behind this interdict? What was the tone of this feast, what was its atmosphere, what excesses did it give rise to? Everything is possible, for there is something violent in these exuberant festivities, an outlet for pent-up desires and social or sexual jealousies, a collective delirium with a purgative effect, like a long nocturnal dream that makes up for the frustrations of daytime.

We know, for example, that one of the important stages of the festivity was the sacrifice of a bull and 11 pigs, which were thrown from the top of the campanile. This was said to be a commemoration of the victory won in 1162 over the city of Aquileia, whose patriarch and 11 of its councillors were shown mercy *in extremis* by the Pope. We may also see sacrifice as a bloody way of celebrating the 'farewell to flesh' – the literal meaning of the word 'carnival' which originally corresponded to the abstention from meat dictated by Lent. As for being a farewell, it was, rather, a period of temporary liberation during which the pleasures of the flesh were permitted.

While today's Carnival, a vast masquerade for tourists that the Venetians shun, lasts for 11 days, just before Shrove Tuesday, we must not forget that at its peak in the 18th century it spread unofficially over half the year! Wearing a mask wasn't just a mere whim, but an obligation. In short, everything was permitted (apart from bearing arms and entering churches), so long as you were masked. Prostitutes would parade around with their breasts bared and their faces covered: the body doesn't have to put up with the same moral restrictions once it is anonymous. The body can take its revenge on the omnipotence of spiritual values, in a vast movement of emancipatory transgression.

The Carnival, in short, is the world upside down, with the poor disguised as the rich, the rich slumming it, false priests and bawdy nuns, women dressed as men, men taken for a walk by dogs themselves disguised as men, and so on, in an interminable sarabande bordering on madness. The best known of the revellers is, of course, Casanova, who took a malicious satisfaction in enjoying his pleasures in the convents, right outside the grille of the parlours, where crimson-faced young nuns had the right to take part, or at least to watch.

How could a government that was in other ways so strict tolerate such uncontrollable merry-making? Certain people will put forward the 'pressure cooker' explanation, suggesting that the festivities which seem to promote disorder act as a safety valve, ultimately guaranteeing security and good social order. Others (and this is an enticing explanation) maintain that the carnival principle is similar to that of gambling, intrinsically linked to the soul of Venice.

As we have already noted, Venice was an impossible wager both architecturally and historically. Throughout the Middle Ages, and even later, the unequalled economic power of the city rested on maritime trade. And what was this trafficking of merchandise between the four corners of the world if not a gigantic lottery? You bet on a particular ship. If it comes back, your fortune is made. If it sinks, you're back at the starting point: you need to invest again, and double your stake. What else can you do, once you are left on the quayside, except cross your fingers and trust in your lucky star? There is some strategy involved, of course, but the rest is up to chance. Thus the notion of chance forms an essential part of the economic system. So why should anyone be astonished that gambling is rooted in the city's most ancient traditions?

In Venice, people gambled everywhere – in the streets, in the salons, in the harbour. But they did so secretly as for a long time it was prohibited. The only exception was one that a mariner cunningly obtained in 1173. At this time, it had just been decided that two columns would be erected on St Mark's Square. But how? The engineers were stumped. There the columns lay, in bits and pieces, on the ground. Sarcasms poured forth. What use are brilliant monuments if they just lie there like poorly-trained guard dogs? So the Doge made a public announcement offering a big reward to anyone who could come up with a solution. A mariner stepped forward. What about raising the shafts with the aid of damp ropes that would then contract once they started to dry? It was a clever idea. And it worked! So what reward would the mariner request? No pieces of gold: just the right to set up a gaming table between the two columns. The astute man foresaw how much he could earn through operating a monopoly gambling concession. The Doge was obliged to accept. Uproar ensued. Where would it all end, if gambling were tolerated right on St Mark's Square? But the mariner had met with someone even more cunning than himself: the Doge decided to make of this site, between the two columns, the place where the heads of those sentenced to death would be exhibited. The spot became accursed, and the mariner, beaten, finally abandoned his privilege.

So if the wild passion for gambling gripped the city, like the sea water seeping between the paving stones of the basilica, ready to rush in once the sluice gates were opened, it would be several centuries before it could emerge into daylight. The spread of card games, at the end of the 16th century, merely accelerated the vogue. Merchants soon realised that there were quicker and more efficient ways of winning a lot of money than by gambling on ships: they could sometimes win (or lose) as much in a single evening as they could in a seafaring excursion. Whether the government authorised it or not, gambling fever spread without limits. The nobles became passionately devoted to this sport which gave them such a shiver of excitement. Wealthy traders were ruined in an evening, the poor suddenly became wealthy, women went so far as to gamble their own bodies away. It was carnival on a grand scale, with the city being transformed into a gigantic gambling den.

This was why, in 1626, the Grand Council took an unprecedented decision: it opened the first public gaming house. It was called Il Ridotto, and was situated in the palazzo San Moisè, in the calle del Ridotto. Just as prostitutes were not forbidden, but merely obliged to wear yellow, gambling was henceforth authorised, but within a very limited territory. Without Venice there would never have been Las Vegas: la Serenissima had just invented the casino.

An enormous crowd thronged there: not just gamblers, but also men, women and children came flocking into the various rooms in the palace, intent on seeing, chatting, meeting, encountering courtesans, having a drink of hot chocolate or enjoying a cold cut of meat. All wearing their masks. It was here, of course, that Casanova would take his conquests, when he wasn't there to make new ones. "Living and gambling are one and the same," people would say, and we shouldn't forget it. This would seem to have been the opinion of a good number of Venetians. In any case, travellers from every land flocked to see the phenomenon. A Scot, John Law, would remain famous for having put into practice here (with great effect) his new knowledge of applied mathematics...

As for the word 'casino', it designates, in Italian, the little house (*casa*) possessed in Venice, as a kind of *pied-à-terre*, by every wealthy proprietor whose main dwelling was in his villa on *terra firma*. It was in these apartments, soon transformed into private clubs, that the passion for gambling survived when the Ridotto, accused of disturbing social order, was finally closed in 1774. Although clandestine, the activity lost none of its liveliness, even if its links with organised prostitution became ever closer, which meant it lost some of its initial playful dimension. As for the Carnival, it was forbidden by the Austrians in 1798, after seven centuries of festivity, only to be reborn, as a municipal initiative, in 1979, thus probably constituting the biggest tourist attraction ever dreamt up.

So Venice was the inventor of the fork, the ghetto, the casino and mass tourism. To that list we can also add lace-making and the famous 'air stitch' developed on the island of Burano. And Fortuny fabrics, famous throughout the world: only three people, it is said, still know the secret of how to make them. Crystal glass too, the first really transparent glass, as well as aventurine, that glass with its coppery shimmer that seems spangled with gold, and chalcedony, which imitates precious stones so well, and even mirror glass – the fabulous contrivance of the master glaziers of Murano, of course. Venice invented the gondola, naturally, that strange, asymmetrical, flat-bottomed boat that only finds its balance when bearing the weight of its rower – like the city itself? Venice invented publishing – well, more or less, since it obtained, in the 16th century, a monopoly of printing as invented by Gutenberg, and perfected a new technique for manufacturing paper, replacing water with gum. It was one of the first cities in Europe to open public paying theatres, with the opera in pride of place: in the era of Monteverdi and Vivaldi, there were over 1,200 operas written and performed in less than a century! The list of Venetian innovations is a long one.

In the middle of the Campo San Zanipolo rises the equestrian statue of the famous Captain Bartolomeo Colleoni, nicknamed 'il Colleone' because he had three testicles. The man was so filled with pride that he had demanded, offering an important bequest at his death in return, that a statue of himself be erected 'before Saint Mark'. The city of the doges, avid for gain but little inclined to encouraging self-aggrandisement, got round his request by setting up the statue in front of the Scuola San Marc; and it was as he gazed at it, they say, that Nietzsche arrived at his theory of the *Übermensch*.

Now, isn't this the thing that best suits this extraordinary city – the myth of the superman? It is a sort of 'super-city' which surpassed all others and, even today, eroded by the high tides and by time, by pollution from the oil tankers of Porto Marghera, by invasions of insects, seaweed and tourists, and deserted by its longstanding families, it is not only still standing, on the shifting soil, amidst the striped sugar-candy pillars to which cling almost ghostly patches of fog, but above all it has kept its leading position in the hit parade of dreams, and is the top destination in the world for lovers. A city born from a dream has become a formidable dream machine.

Venice
& the Carnival

But what a shame I didn't come here when I was a younger man, when I was full of daring!

Claude Monet

Of all the places where the Carnival was most facetious in the days of yore, for dance, and song, and serenade, and ball. And masque, and mime, and mystery, and more than I have time to tell now, or at all, Venice the bell from every city bore, – And at the moment when I fix my story, that sea-horn was in all her glory.

Lord Byron

…he saw it once more, that most astonishing of
all landing-places, that dazzling composition of
fantastic architecture which the Republic
presented to the admiring gaze of approaching
seafarers: the unburdened splendour of the
Ducal Palace, the Bridge of Sighs, the lion and
the saint on their two columns at the water's
edge, the vista beyond it of the gate tower and
the Giant's Clock; and as he contemplated it all
he reflected that to arrive in Venice by land, at
the station, was like entering a palace by a back
door: that only now as he was doing by ship,
over the high sea, should one come to this most
extraordinary of cities.

Thomas Mann
Death in Venice

A ghost upon the sands of the sea, so weak – so quiet, – so bereft of all but her loveliness, that we might well doubt, as we watched her faint reflection in the mirage of the lagoon, which was the City, and which the shadow.

John Ruskin
The Stones of Venice

Can there be anyone who has not had to overcome a fleeting sense of dread, a secret shudder of uneasiness, on stepping for the first time or after a long interval of years into a Venetian gondola? How strange a vehicle it is, coming down unchanged from times of old romance, and so characteristically black, the way no other thing is black except a coffin – a vehicle evoking lawless adventures in the splashing stillness of night, the last silent journey!

Thomas Mann
Death in Venice

Michael R Lucas

Michael Lucas was born in Surrey, England in 1948. He studied engineering at London Polytechnic College and in 1986 moved to San Francisco where he founded his own firm. In the meantime, he has pursued his passion for photography, being active in several photographic clubs, and also the Audubon Society. Working mostly in the landscape genre, his pictures are highly sought-after by photo agencies.

Bibliography

Horatio F. Brown, *Venetian Studies*, K. Paul, Trench & Co., London, 1887.

Lord Byron, *The Poetical Works of Lord Byron*, edited by Ernest Hartley Coleridge, John Murray, London, 1905.

Thomas Mann, *Death in Venice & other stories*, translated and with an introduction by David Luke, Vintage, London, 1998.

John Ruskin, *The Stones of Venice*, Penguin, London, 2001.